ON THE LONG BLUE NIGHT

ELIOT
CARDINAUX

DOS MADRES

2023

DOS MADRES PRESS INC.
P.O. Box 294, Loveland, Ohio 45140
www.dosmadres.com   editor@dosmadres.com

Dos Madres is dedicated to the belief that the small press is essential
to the vitality of contemporary literature as a carrier of the new voice,
as well as the older, sometimes forgotten voices of the past. And in an
ever more virtual world, to the creation of fine books pleasing to the
eye and hand.

Dos Madres is named in honor of Vera Murphy and Libbie Hughes,
the "Dos Madres" whose contributions have made this press possible.

Dos Madres Press, Inc. is an Ohio Not For Profit Corporation and a
501 (c) (3) qualified public charity. Contributions are tax deductible.

Executive Editor: Robert J. Murphy

Illustration & Book Design: Elizabeth H. Murphy
www.illusionstudios.net

Typeset in Adobe Garamond Pro
ISBN 978-1-953252-85-2
Library of Congress Control Number: 2023940610

ACKNOWLEDGMENTS

Some of these poems first appeared in *Jacket2*, and *Talisman*. My sincere thanks to the editors.

Some of these poems first appeared on the albums *Out of Our Systems*, *A Living Past*, and *What the Wildflower Witnessed* (Our Hearts as Thieves). My deep thanks to the musicians who brought them to life.

I have been extremely fortunate in my readers. My gratitude to Peter Gizzi, Patrick Pritchett, and Cynthia Cruz.

This book would not exist but for the mentorship of Peter Gizzi, Ivy Schweitzer, Michael Tillyer, and Ruth Lepson. My most heartfelt thanks.

I also owe a debt of gratitude to Pierre Joris, for his foundational translations of Paul Celan.

All my love to family, blood or no.

Merci merci merci

For Jan & Christina van Wijk

TABLE OF CONTENTS

ON THE LONG BLUE NIGHT

Endnote: Poetry "a shrine with no temple"

—Paul Celan, *Microliths*

PAUL CELAN
BENEATH THE ASPEN TREE

Offerings in Originarity

In the lateword an earwig
crawls
out of childhood wide
intelligence o
soundless body

What makes you
write this I heard
in the octaves a night prayer go
also gratefully away

You say what
it was the first thing
before birth

We can hold & deal with
tension give
what it means to
create to
vanish the window
between us

Unspeaking the human project
blacken without
being named

Lying in the House of You

I. The Silent

Cold fire: the
wolves' eyes flicker
into no one's language.

II. The Victors

Rain stings the pulse
of the fields we lie in.
Stare loudly into the flames.

III. The Named

Torn from the flowerless rose
I have a single thorn of light
to carve their constellation.

IV. The Lost

I am a stranger, & this is their bread.
The knife is a sky between us.
Break it with your hands

V. The Hungry

The crater's wheat is holy.
A whole spent earth
rises mutely over the rim.

VI. The Defeated

My heart still frightened
eases the grasses, lying
in the house of you.

Goya

The ladder sinks rung by rung
into thunder's echo.
Flutes bite the silence.
The fang & the flower
ossify,

   horse
   falling off
   the bone.

  All animals
& their human souls
break into captivity.

The sun slowly covers the mask.

For Osip Mandelstam

Lightlid, you tenderly shed
what soft & flaring
black sunbeams
bled to become.

The Jessamine's
five suns faded
        translucent as wax,

or the pale noon sun
of elsewhere
        embraced by brambles.

Those witness, the mourners
& those
        who attended the vigil

unsafe in the light of candles
even the acme of a twisted smile
longs to embrace, but can't unmake.

& the red glare of sacrifice
finally forever
        begins to silence

those parched singers;
never in my life
have I heard such music.

Paul Celan Beneath the Aspen Tree

I.
See,
those knifecords —

a knot in the blood
overblown with margins
at that

enclosure —
wolfskinned.

Witness,
wisteria blowing
deep

into matter
& deeper.

II.
Finch,
the lymph node swells
in the bark,

beneath it;
your translucent
hammertrunk,
it sleeps through the keyhole.

What the way,
hacks-through,
hacks-into,
the throat can give,
maybe weighs: this
branch.

III.
Take these trimmings —

of whose shadow,
to whom
        I belong,

round as a month
or a lunar

mouth's-word —
at mouth's-worth.

Horse-fetched
or Time-lent
still,

do they
flutter & bray?

IV.
Excess,
the torpor-outridden —
the more-than-
stupor,
outrid
of its other,
my unaware,

distranslated
melancholy
breadmaker.

Bloodsucking second
hand-darkened,
of the pleat-enfolding
matterstopped tongue,
begun to rewind;
its thoughts,
blurted.

V.
The thrice-flayed,
thrice-frayed leaf
in the mantle
of the stem

clearquestions
the ground-
gap;

that shrieking,
idiot
glory,
when

will it speak?
Tomorrow-
after.

VI.
Memory, two rooms away:
her bitter stems drinking

salt water from eyes
of Galilee.

Honey, the bees
made of our bodies,

lying there
two rooms away.

VII.
Trauma,
that blindness, that
lavender metal,

innocence
crouched like a wound
& its hollowed-out

double,
everthinking
mindbramblestorm.

Look, the way it
holds still.

VIII.
One day I too will write you,
no letter to say,
this one,
true thing:

to rotate
beyond, behind
the eyefilm,

mantlebranched:
your word.

THERE IS A PLACE FOR HELL
IN ALL OF US

Sigil

For Sean Ali

Shadows of
sunset under eyelids
hover over sleep.
I grieve my splinter out.

The wind made a lap
in the heart. In the iris
a reel flaps with bright
white birdsong.

Precipitation

Initiate first
the grey-green weather

First pocket of sky
escaped from underneath
your tongue

Then the white of the sun
on a word like "steel"
will forget us

A shudder of heat
at the root of your shadow

The lightless lilt
of untranslated cloud

To keep the salt
from skimming
sunskins of memory

Undisclosing
day

Last Fall

I.
It was how I decayed
that hurt you

I left my body
on the roof

& with your eyes
you felt my shell
in the morning light

& then like an apple
I lost my shape
one day

II.
It wasn't you
I know exactly how you feel that way

The sun came up
& the sun came down

You left my
body on the roof
under falling snow
& abrasive heat

III.
Small voice in weather
if you can die
now
      knowing no less of it

A dry hollow
sound of
having fallen

Agony

An hour of
silence

& a falling sound

IV.
It was how
I decayed that
hurt you

How you
left my body

How it changed one day

& you touched me through the window with your
eyes

Daily Become Human Again

For Isabel Duarte-Gray

Clutter of branches
in public,
indifferent
language
      of a bleak sky

Won't you take what is given,
pain in the branches
ringing the gavel,
cradled like a lamb

The whole
      stretching out
in a blanket of tears,
a corporeal fugue

After I Begged Myself

I.
There is a place for hell in all of us

We look up to where all of you is

Impossible
not to believe in
an atmosphere
every particle can touch & is

Synthetic
gesture to reality

II.
The pain of a body
expended

Excesses of
courage & strength

I love this language

Love it madly

Here it is

I Walk Each Day

Along these walls

I set
up a defeated
country

Even briefly
insane

I'm loved
by these walls

Their shadows faint
& harmless

I walk each day

The acorns push disaster

Furnish our living space

These walls
can move

Someone's pain
is confined by this

The sky is a final
fevered blue

Where chaos laid
a hand on them

Host

& fighting them off
I eat of this
alongside others
hoping to identify

The wound & its landscape
sharpness on every
tongue
      I keep it
      for myself
      let me
            eat of it
                  again

& death will measure
patience
      as long as I live

& carry on
uncaring
incarnation
carrion in
bloom

THE EXILE DREAMS
OF EXODUS

The Exile Dreams of Exodus

Lifting the edge
of a wound while
a white cross burns.

A little red flag.
In sunlight, a sickness of bees
agitating the dark

rippling nectar of
autumn. Meridians wander
through untouched lands.

The stage pursues
the actor, now.
It drives me through my birthplace.

Coming of Age

In the newspaper of the future
wounds were read by
light cast on the sky.

A papercut stemmed,
low tide, a clock
inherited an airstrike.

A handshake,
hour of my birthplace,
enclosed a bee.

I rage at the sky in blue,
an angel of the county
beheaded; a golf club.

In the splinters of a deck
the lovers entangled
imagine their own apartment.

Apologia

Never
traversing your
city, I wore

the unwishing
cloudscowl

snowscuffing
your master

wreathing
a falsified winter.

Along came
one sky-
flawed snare-
roll, lift-
ing
   confetti of fear

on a breath of
horsehair.

False Door

For Jade

I walk through poetry out into the world.
I have forgotten something, maybe

my coat. I have just woken up.
I go on a walk with poetry, looking for a door.

You tell me it is there, looking onto our bedroom.
It needs a poem.

I need to make my way through something.
I could go on a walk with you.

I could hear the exile singing.

Something's New

Like, now

Like the dream of a newly naked city come
spring when it rains and the marigolds hatch
in the minds of birds, it won't still the soft
trappings of flutter and ache, light and swell

Like the prose of an exile's house flowing
into white linens, slips & sheets in the
southbound wind, when this ruptures &
shrapnels your shoulder into woodgrain

Feuilles (Leaving)

Heart

Blown through like
leaves

Obscured

Let the dark minor ring
against a distance

Along unnoticed

Outward

Designs
of frustration

Useless

Given
to fusing

Absence

Dwelling
in abrasion

Noiselessly
considers you

Red,

Was it you
who danced

With some
subtracted
sense

Wheeled-
about,

Un-
spoken

Who Ripped Out
My Romantic Heart & Said

You might enjoy this
eventually

My particular brand of
madness

He

He

He

Dark shit

Nosferatu

Of the free world

But to die of your own hand

Without lifting a knife

Who did you strangle
for such a place in things

For Osip Mandelstam II

I remember you caught me
looking up at the blossoms.
They fell like skirts on my thighs,
and I still see the color
violet, burning through my chest.

I carry my history blind, like a shame.
I drag it like a weapon behind me.

I lay these things down for the first time
in a grave beside your image,
saying these things out loud.

ON THE LONG BLUE NIGHT

Toward Truth or Consequence

For Monica Jane Frisell

I.
Was I
the landscape
emptied

Husk I am
filled with things I eat

To make room for you
who looked away
& confirmed my secret

Things allowed
but that grew
too quickly

To catch
up between my own
& I

This bustle of standing
still

II.
I do not believe this
power

Nothing
I can control

A catalog
of empty friends

A field
& a landscape of brush

Come out with me

A ghost I would
& could not drink of

A body
slipping at midday

Slow death we lead
this life

& the most emptied
street

III.
Unhindered crocus

Unlike the decade
lay grey on the couch
& unable to speak

Striking
against the wages
of tomorrow
like a bell

All
us & we

All you
& I

& our distance from them

In fury & revery

Time Emptied of Us

I.
& work upended

Loss of speech

As with everything's shadows

Hovered like heat

II.
In perfect
invocative silence

Hearing the blood beat

Movement
in absolute motionless
absence grew
toward us
as if we were suns

III.
I'll focus on something else

What the sky can be

What a tree can do

A redbud

Baby blue

IV.
What the mourning doves say

The cat leaves its shadow
like language
everywhere

Fruit

Shame is almost rebellious

Seeds & glaciers
move

Shaking
trees of their robins

Adherent
to gravity

Tremors
in buried wind

We sparkle
antithetically

Is that the Mercy
or the Psalm

The pain we wake to
rooted in the flaw

Birds raining abject
onto the earth

Voices in
green mesh

Hearts nesting in
camouflage

Rose in
honeysuckle

What the fuck
happened here

Amends

I.
Where are you, drift?
How much is buried.
What is deep in snow.

The eye hears echoes
& is led

There's nothing lying there

You stand here & put it
in their hands

The drift is nearness
crying

If you can stand time,
in it

No temple around me

There I shrine
beginning

II.
Lord, why have I come for you

No reason

Not-Unexpected Feeling

(The Lovers)

Three very
personable people
sitting near me

On a picnic bench

Talking
animatedly

Probably about
what's going on

I'm thinking

Alcohol is a machine
it

Analyzes me
it

Turns me on like

A machine

It has control of me
right now

But only barely

Barely

Just
between dark & dreaming

Did I say
enough

My thoughts won't
linger
in the fields

Tomorrow I will walk them

No

But soon

I know someday
this light will vanish

I'll
walk them to where it opens
on the long blue night

Talk of Ghosts

I didn't know

Maybe would hurt
from excitement
falling today

I didn't know
I would title something
after something Ingrid said
& that we shared
this feeling

I knew it
only when she said it
that we shared it

Knew only later
what it meant
& how far it was shared

& now I am writing this
I believe I will forget it again
not knowing how to touch
on the word *striking*
unspeakable silence
hovering around a wound

You cannot read some books
except in silence
& you can
not write some poems
without music

This is a ghost town with people
walking it

What dialect is
that silence
carving out

That could never be right
how to leave it alone

There are so many ways
of doing wrong now
saying you understand
asking if you
wonder at the light
when it does not touch you
warming me in comfort
where I do not notice

ABOUT THE AUTHOR

 ELIOT CARDINAUX was born in Dayton, Ohio in 1984, and spent time growing up in Geneva, Switzerland. In addition to being a poet and translator, he is a pianist and composer working in the field of jazz and improvisation. He studied briefly at Manhattan School of Music, and Conservatorium van Amsterdam, before completing his degree in music at New England Conservatory. He went on to acquire an MFA in poetry from The University of Massachusetts Amherst. He has traveled to Denmark and Germany several times over the last decade to perform and record his poetry and music. Eliot has collaborated with Asger Thomsen, Mat Maneri, Taus Bregnhøj-Olesen, Randy Peterson, Tristan Honsinger, Axel Dörner, Jeb Bishop, Herb Robertson, Jaimie Branch, Joe Morris, Ed Schuller, Flin van Hemmen, Jonas Engel, Etienne Nillesen, Tony Malaby, Thomas Morgan, Kresten Osgood, Mia Dyberg, Zoe Christiansen, Isaac Luxon, Eivind Opsvik, Katya Popova, Peter Knapp, Ryan Blotnick, Sean Ali, and many others. At present, he has a trio with Will McEvoy and Max Goldman, a duo with Gary Fieldman, and is a member of the international ensemble Our Hearts as Thieves. His albums include *American Thicket*, *Sweet Beyond Witness*, *Out of Our Systems*, and *Pavane*. He is the founder of The Bodily Press, an independent chapbook press and record label. He has taught at UMass Amherst, and worked as a bookseller at Amherst Books.

Author photograph by Asger Thomsen